HARLOW'S PONIES

This book belongs to

....

HARLOW'S PONIES

Contents

HARLOW'S PONIES

Published by DJ Murphy (Publishers) Ltd, Olive Studio, Grange Road, Tilford, Farnham, Surrey GU10 2DQ

Who did what in Harlow Yearbook 2025

Devised and created by Harlow Luna White, Sarah Burgess, Louise Kittle
Design Sarah Garland, Lucy Claydon
Photography Chelsea White, Equinational Photography, LRG Photography, shutterstock.com
Managing Director Zoe Cannon
Commercial Director Abi Cannon

Harlow Yearbook is produced under license by DJ Murphy (Publishers) Ltd.

Printed in Italy by Rotolito S.p.A.

ISBN 978-1-913787-29-5

RRP £12.99

All about...
POPCORN

Get to know Popcorn – the main man, the OG and forever my heart horse!

PONY PROFILE

- **BREED**
  Part-bred Welsh
- **HEIGHT**
  13.2hh
- **COLOUR**
  Palomino
- **BIRTHDAY**
  9 June 2006

Ideal day...

Popcorn's ideal day involves going adventuring somewhere new! There's nothing better than zoomies through the countryside, and when he knows we're off for a gallop, he gets so excited! His ears are pricked and rather than being Mr Cool, he's up on his toes, ready to go!

Dream job...

He would 100% be a model in another life – there is no doubt about that! Popcorn's literally the dream pony on photoshoots. He just stands there with his ears forward, and sometimes he even turns his head in the same direction as me. We're so in sync!

Favourite memory...

My best memory with Popcorn has to be our first time riding on the beach. We live really nearby, but I'd never taken a pony there before. It had always been a dream of mine to gallop along the sand, and the sky was incredible! I'll never ever forget that day.

What makes him happy...

The thing that makes Popcorn happiest is treats! I mean, who doesn't love treats?! But he definitely thinks with his tummy. And pretty much anything goes... carrots, apples, mints, Stud Muffins, tasty licks... the list goes on. He really does love them all!

SIMPLE SCHOOLING

Supercharge your sessions with my great guide!

5 EXERCISES TO TRY...

- [ ] Square halts – a halt is required at the end of every dressage test, so perfecting them is key! Encouraging your pony to stand politely for a few seconds is also good for his handling, too.
- [ ] Riding without stirrups can feel wobbly, but take it steady and your position will improve loads! Remember to stay relaxed, though, and hold a neck strap for balance if you need to, rather than leaning on your pony's mouth – ouch!
- [ ] Shallow loops are fab for testing suppleness and can be ridden in walk, trot or canter. You can make them more challenging by increasing the depth, too!
- [ ] Transitions – working on lots of different kinds will help make your pony responsive to your aids! Have a go at progressive ones, such as walk to trot, as well as direct ones, such as walk to canter.
- [ ] Lateral moves require your pony to move forwards and sideways at the same time, how fancy?! You'll need to be completely co-ordinated with your aids, so ask your instructor to show you how to do it.

THE LOWDOWN

Schooling is all about improving your riding, teaching your pony new skills and boosting his way of going. During your sessions, spend time working on the flatwork fundamentals – these include straightness, suppleness, balance, responsiveness and rhythm!

Seeing the progress we've made is so rewarding

4 TOP TIPS...

Use your space – no matter where you're schooling, don't stick to one small corner or the track. Moving around helps make sure your pony is paying attention to what you're asking.

Mix up your sessions by adding in poles! Polework is amazing for your pony, so throw in some different layouts – there's loads of inspo online!

Work your pony equally on each rein to keep his muscles even. If he struggles in one direction, speak to an adult for advice as he might need a check-up.

Think about your position during your session, from your head to your toes. It will influence the effectiveness of your aids, too!

3 PLACES TO SCHOOL YOUR PONY...

In the arena – this is the safest place, so will fill you with confidence! It can really help improve your accuracy, too, as you'll have markers to guide you – essential for dressage tests!

On grass – this is a must if you plan to event or show your pony. Grass is often a bit more slippery than an arena surface, so practice helping your pony improve his balance, especially on turns.

Out hacking – if your pony's more energetic and responsive on a hack than in the arena, make the most of it by riding some lateral moves down a bridlepath or doing medium trot up a hill!

2 THINGS TO THINK ABOUT...

Setting an aim for each session will make it super productive. It's not much fun for you or your pony to just trot and canter round in circles aimlessly, so add some structure to your sessions.

Always try to finish on a good note and reward your pony with a gentle scratch on his neck for doing well. It's better to have a short, positive session!

HEARD IT FROM HARLOW

The great thing about schooling is that you can wear whatever riding outfit you want! But I always try to look smart for my sessions because it makes me feel fab and I'm sure I ride better because of it!

1 THING I LOVE...

Seeing the progress we've made during a schooling session is so rewarding, whether it's something as simple as riding a seamless walk-trot transition or perfecting a trickier move!

CRISS-CROSS

Have a go at completing this cool criss-cross puzzle!

Four letters
Rolo

Five letters
White
Panda
Welsh

Six letters
Harlow
Cloudy
Family
Harlen

Seven letters
Chelsea
Jumping
Showing
Popcorn
Dressage

Eight letters
Dartmoor
Shetland

Nine letters
Competing
Connemara

How did you do?

Head to p100 to check your answers!

Squad goals! Nothing makes me happier than hanging out with my amazing ponies!

TRIP OF A LIFETIME

I love looking back at pics from our safari

The White Family absolutely love travelling, and we've been on some pretty epic adventures together, but I'm not sure how we'll top our incredible South Africa safari! It was sooo special going away just me and Mum, and an experience I'll definitely remember forever.

HEARD IT FROM HARLOW

We wore neutral-coloured riding clothes so we were better camouflaged out riding, which made it easier to get closer to the animals!

The Big Five!

The reserve we stayed on had so many incredible animals to spot, including rhino, who like to break into the stables area to steal the hay! There were no elephants or lions, though, so we went on a sunset drive to a nearby reserve, where we saw them, and even a spotted hyena – super rare!

Ticking off the Big Five!

It was an experience I'll remember forever

ALARM CALL

We got up really early to ride before it was too hot, but I'm used to that with showing. Relaxing by the pool after was pretty fun, too!

BONDING TIME!

I loved heading down to the stables to help bring in the horses and groom and tack up – it helped me miss my boys a bit less!

No biggie, just riding with a giraffe!

LOOK AFTER YOUR PONY'S...
MANE AND TAIL

Give your pony's hair some TLC and he'll have luscious locks in no time

Like us, every pony's hair is different – some have naturally neat manes that sit perfectly to one side (Popcorn, that's you!) and others will have manes that just can't be tamed (I'm looking at you, Cloudy boy!). But whatever type of hair your pony has, it's important to take care of it.

After all, his mane and tail does more than just make him look fabulous!

HEARD IT FROM HARLOW

When Rolo goes showing, his mane and tail are left natural because he's native. I absolutely love how perfectly his long mane flows in the breeze – goals!

No flaky bits in there, Cloudy!

1. To give your pony's mane a check over and good spruce up, grab a soft brush (a body brush will do!), comb, mane and tail brush, and some detangling spray.

2. Carefully feel through your pony's mane and tail, focusing on the roots and looking for any dry, flaky skin. You can use the comb to help separate the hair and get a good look.

3. Use a soft brush to remove any dirt that's stuck in your pony's mane and tail. Avoid overbrushing, especially with a hard brush, as it will break the hairs.

THE LOWDOWN

Ponies use their tails to swish the flies away! In summer, you might see ponies in a herd standing nose to tail – they do this to help keep the bugs away from their pals, how cute!

4. Pick up your detangler and give the mane and tail a good spray, being careful to avoid getting it on your pony's back – you don't want to make his coat slippery!

5. Brush through his hair until the knots are gone and it's silky smooth! When doing his tail, hold a small section at a time and brush through gently to prevent pulling – ouch!

Totally tangle-free... for now!

HEARD IT FROM HARLOW

To prevent the boy's from getting grubby tails when travelling, I plait them and pop on a special tail bag.

Hair salon

Washing your pony's mane and tail every now and again will help it stay healthy. Use a pony-friendly shampoo, then a conditioner to nourish and soften it!

When it comes to tidying his locks, it's best to ask an adult to help. But, depending on your pony's breed and type, a good trim can make all the difference to his overall look.

Hair gloss – perfect finishing touch!

THE LOWDOWN

Some ponies have naturally straight hair, whereas others have slightly curly or frizzy locks! If you want your pony to rock a beach wave vibe, you could plait his mane and leave it in for a day. It'll look so cute!

Essential protection

To help prevent your pony's mane from being rubbed, look for rugs that have a special silky lining, or you can try using a close-fitting lycra hood! They can help protect the mane, as well as keep your pony clean pre-comp – how ideal!

Keeping the knots away!

"Cloudy's fluffy blond mane definitely adds to his personality!"

HEARD IT FROM HARLOW

Traditionally a pony's mane should lie on the right, and this is important in showing classes! If your pony's mane sits on the left, you can train it over by plaiting it down to the right.

HORSE PLAY

RIDING WITH OTHERS

One of the best things about riding is that you can enjoy it with your friends!

GOSSIP GIRL

Hacking in company is one of my fave things to do when. It means the ponies can have a good blast and I can catch up with friends! Sometimes we get a bit over-excited and start singing songs or making up crazy stories – it's so funny!

IN SYNC

Drill riding is sooo much fun! Riding side-by-side to practise a dressage test, or making up a routine full of fancy moves to our fave playlist – it's always hilarious performing it to Mum!

SWITCH IT UP

I have learnt so much from riding different ponies – and that includes epic Grand Prix horses, as well as my boys, who are all sooo different! Pony swapping with friends is a great way to boost your skills, plus you can give each other advice to make the most of your sessions!

TRUTH OR DARE

Even though some are totally mad, I'm always so up for doing riding dares and I love getting requests from my followers for the videos. So why don't you have a go at some of my fave dares with your friends? Tacking up blindfolded, cantering with no hands or jumping with no stirrups – there's so many to try!

TWINNING

You know I love matching with my ponies, but what about matching with your riding pals and their ponies, too?! That's the ultimate matchy-matchy vibe!

THE LOWDOWN

Ponies are super-sociable, but remember – like people – not all ponies get along. So, when riding with others, look out for any signs that show your pony's unhappy, such as ears back or tail swishing.

On schedule

A day in the life of the herd at home

At the beginning of 2024, all our dreams came true when we moved into a house that had land for the ponies. Here's what the boys get up to on a typical day at home...

Wakey wakey

It's 7am and time for the ponies to have breakfast! There's nothing quite like walking out the back door and seeing the ponies first thing in the morning. It's sooo cute when they greet me with a whinny!

Get dressed

While the ponies are munching on their breakfast, they have a change of clothes so they're ready for the field. The rugs the ponies wear depends on the time of year and weather, so in winter this job can take a lot longer!

Once they've finished eating and are dressed, I turn them out in their paddocks for the day.

Stable spruce up

Now the ponies are out of the way, it's time to get going with the mucking out! It's not the most glam job, but I love giving them a fresh, fluffy bed ready for when they come in later.

This is also when I clean out their water buckets, make haynets and prepare feeds for dinner and the next morning. Getting all the jobs done in one go saves loads of time!

HEARD IT FROM HARLOW

I try to prepare everything for a show the day before, but it can be exhausting when it's an early start because we have to get up even earlier to feed so they have time to digest breakfast before we leave!

HEARD IT FROM HARLOW

Seeing the ponies lie down and being able to enjoy more cuddles is the best! Plus, I don't have to harass Mum about taking me to the yard any more – eveyone's a winner!

Time for a workout

The ponies usually get exercised in the afternoon after I've finished school – unless we're off to a comp or training, or it's the school holidays!

I try to vary their routines as much as possible to keep things interesting, so I'll mix it up throughout the week so they all have schooling sessions, a little jump, plenty of hacking and some groundwork, as well as a day or two off.

Back to bed

The ponies come in from the field as late as possible as I want them to have as much freedom as they can!

Once they're in, they have their feet picked out, a quick groom and check over, and rugs on for the night.

Before I go to bed I do a night check to make sure they've got enough water and hay. And obviously give them lots of cuddles and kisses!

HEARD IT FROM HARLOW

It's hard work having the ponies at home, especially during term time, but it's so much fun and I feel like my bond with the boys has grown even stronger!

Meet ROCKET

FACT FILE

- **DATE OF BIRTH**
  10 February 2024
- **BREED**
  English Cream Miniature Dachshund
- **BEST FRIEND**
  Harlen
- **FAVE TREAT**
  Chicken
- **FAVE ACTIVITY**
  Chasing us around the house!
- **BEST COLOUR**
  Baby blue

We're so lucky to have a dog who's as amazing (and beautiful!) as Rocket because he's been the easiest puppy to train! He absolutely loves going on long walks, especially with his big friends – the way he looks up to them is just so sweet, I honestly can't cope!

Apart from walkies and going zoomies around the house, he loves sleeping, too. It's the cutest thing when he's curled up in his snuggly bed!

Silly sausage

It's so funny – and ridiculously cute – when Rocket stretches out his whole body along the carpet like a sausage! He even sticks his legs out behind him to get the full stretch!

His favourite place to be tickled is his tummy. Belly rubs are number one in Rocket's world! When you really get the spot, he rolls over onto his back and kicks his dinky legs in the air. Everything he does is utterly adorable!

Insider info

Rocket has an extensive wardrobe! He's only little so needs all the protection he can get from the mud!

> *Everything Rocket does is utterly adorable!*

HEARD IT FROM HARLOW

When I hold Rocket in my arms to say hello to the ponies, they're so gentle with him! He also loves to sit and watch me from the garden when I'm riding!

HEARD IT FROM HARLOW

All of the training in the dark and cold is so worth it when you achieve your dreams. Trust me, I know!

HARLOW'S

I think these photos will always be my faves. I mean, check out my cheesy grin – you'd be smiling, too, if you'd just qualified for HOYS! I'm so grateful for Rolo and all the amazing things we've done together so far.

HEARD IT FROM HARLOW

This epic sash hangs in my bedroom – isn't it the most amazing thing you've ever seen?!

Aah, Panda pops! When he arrived, I wasn't sure what our future together would be, but he's turned his hoof to everything, including jumping some insane working hunter courses with my coach, Katy, as well as bringing home the ribbons with me! I can't wait to make more memories x

SCRAPBOOK!

HEARD IT FROM HARLOW

It's so much fun loading the boys and heading to a comp – although I need plenty of Percy Pigs to power me through when there's two to ride!

Harlen's riding adventures

Seeing the progress my little brother has made is so special!

Harlen has really got to grips with riding and his confidence is sky rocketing, thanks to my amazing ponies showing him the ropes!

Ready, set, goal!
Harlen's dreams are set on winning a red rosette! He's so competitive, but his skills have improved loads this year and I'm sure it won't be long until he's hanging all his rosettes and sashes up around his bedroom like me!

Time to explore
Hacking is definitely Harlen's favourite riding activity, and he's really confident now so we can go trotting around the fields together!

But, I think when he starts working on his jumping skills, he'll love that even more!

HEARD IT FROM HARLOW

Life feels complete when me, Mum and Harlen get to go hacking together, and now the ponies are at home we get to do it more often!

HEARD IT FROM HARLOW

I need to watch out because Harlen seems to be stealing my ponies! First it was Cloudy, and now he's planning on adding Rolo and Popcorn to his string!

Love and loathe!
I find it so funny how much Harlen loves to clean the ponies' feed buckets! It's super handy, though, because it's an important job and he's really good at getting them sparkling clean!

Harlen actually enjoys most of the yard chores, even the tough ones like mucking out, sweeping and poo picking!

All about... ROLO

Get to know Rolo – the superstar who's made my showing dreams come true!

PONY PROFILE

- **BREED**
  Dartmoor
- **HEIGHT**
  12hh
- **COLOUR**
  Brown
- **BIRTHDAY**
  18 April 2014

Ideal day...

Rolo's dream day has got to involve jumping and water – his two favourite things, apart from flicking his toes in the show ring, of course! He finds splashing around in the water so much fun, especially on a cross-country course where he can jump in and out of it!

Dream job...

Rolo is the quirkiest pony I've ever met, so he'd definitely be a comedian or maybe a circus performer in another life! He's always pulling funny faces and making us laugh with his crazy antics – my fave is when he shows off his perfectly straight, white teeth!

Favourite memory...

There's no doubt about it, my best memory with Rolo has got to be winning at the Royal International. I honestly couldn't believe it when we were called forward into first place – dreams really do come true when you have a pony like Rolo!

What makes him happy...

Rolo's definitely the joker of the herd and he loves sticking his tongue out and throwing his feed bowl around – so cheeky! Entertaining the other ponies is Rolo's fave pastime, and I'm sure they appreciate the banter, too!

HAPPY HACKING

Get set to go on hours of pony adventures with my guide to hacking!

THE LOWDOWN

Hacking is all about exploring with your pony! Riding with friends or by yourself, if an adult says it's okay, is just sooo much fun and will make you feel super-happy!

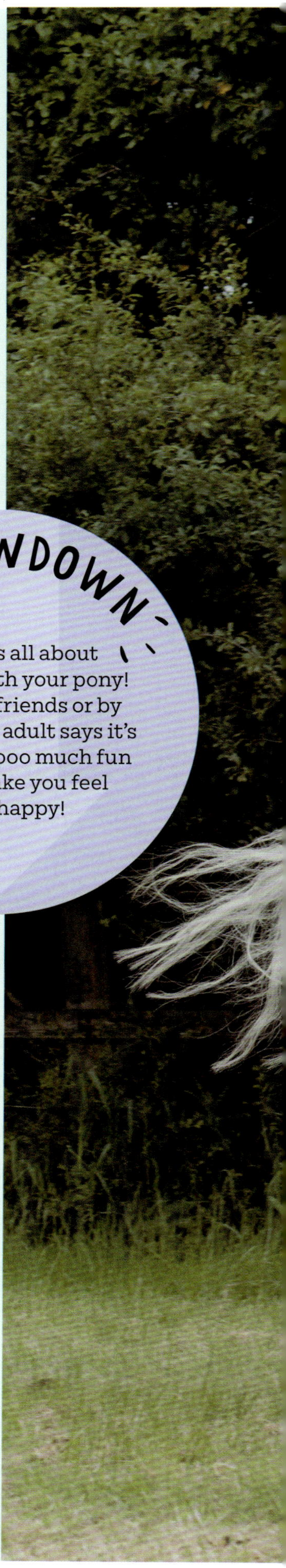

5 THINGS TO KNOW...

Always plan your route and let an adult know where you're going, as well as when you expect to be back. It's a good idea to take a phone with you, too, in case of emergencies!

If your hacking involves riding on the roads, you'll need to swot up on the rules! It's really important to thank other road users who pass you carefully and signal to them where you're going.

Always walk past other horses you meet out hacking. You don't know how they'll react, so give them plenty of room.

When hacking with friends, make sure you communicate with each other to stay safe.

Hacking is great for boosting your pony's confidence and trust in you. Some ponies can be nervous to start – if yours is, ride with an experienced friend who can help you overcome tricky situations.

Hacking is great for boosting your pony's confidence and trust in you

HEARD IT FROM HARLOW

If your local hacking doesn't have much variety, you could load up your pony and take him somewhere new. The world is your oyster!

4 PLACES TO GO...

The beach – dreamy sunrises and a splash in the sea? Yes please!

Woodland – listening to the birds sing as we trot between the trees always makes me feel so chilled.

Open fields – going for a blast on a smooth, grassy track is my fave!

Roads – building the ponies' confidence and boosting their fitness is a must.

3 ACTIVITIES TO TRY...

- [ ] Interval training – this involves periods of low and high intensity work and is amazing for developing your pony's fitness.
- [ ] Schooling – some ponies are a bit spicier and more responsive when hacking, so why not make the most of it and practise your lateral work?
- [ ] Cross-country practise – jump a log, ride through a puddle and canter up hills, they're all skills needed for XC riding!

2 THINGS TO WEAR...

To keep you and your pony safe, it's a good idea to wear brightly-coloured clothing. Popping on a high-vis tabbard is a fab way to help others spot you quickly, too!

Safety gear, such as your riding hat, is essential, but wearing a body protector can help you feel extra confident.

1 THING I LOVE...

There's nothing better than going zoomies! When Popcorn squeals with delight as I pick up two-point position and Rolo's mane whips in the wind as we gallop through the glorious countryside, I always have the biggest grin on my face. It's just the best feeling, especially after a long day at school!

DISCIPLINE DECISIONS

Do you know your disciplines? Complete the clues, then find the answers in the wordsearch!

X	E	E	Z	W	Y	K	R	D	V	I	U	W	J	Q
I	L	S	U	K	U	H	X	A	X	G	A	V	R	Y
A	D	R	E	S	S	A	G	E	C	H	H	O	C	F
H	A	F	B	K	T	Z	U	X	Q	I	I	D	R	N
Z	A	K	H	F	Q	C	N	E	C	K	N	K	O	B
D	G	S	H	O	W	J	U	M	P	I	N	G	S	M
N	P	N	E	N	R	D	R	I	V	I	N	G	S	S
Q	P	I	J	D	R	S	N	R	T	A	L	V	C	H
Z	O	O	L	B	O	Z	E	T	G	L	P	A	O	O
C	Z	Z	L	T	B	W	F	B	Q	E	O	U	U	W
K	R	G	U	O	Q	G	B	I	A	Q	B	L	N	I
V	R	M	Z	D	C	N	J	Y	U	L	N	T	T	N
F	R	A	H	O	H	R	G	F	K	B	L	I	R	G
D	R	F	A	J	T	V	U	U	X	U	O	N	Y	R
X	E	N	D	U	R	A	N	C	E	U	X	G	Y	Q

CLUES!

1

☐

__ __ __ __

involves hitting a ball with a special stick called a mallet from a pony!

2

☐

__ __ __ __ __ __ __ __ __

is a form of racing but over a long distance!

3

☐

__ __ __ __ __ __ __ __ __

is like rugby on horseback and it looks sooo fun!

4

☐

__ __ __ __ __ __

is when a group of horses or ponies go as fast as they can to win!

5

☐

Power, control and accuracy is required in

__ __ __ __ __ __ __ __ __ __ __

to get a clear round!

6

☐

__ __ __ __ __ __ __ __

is like gymnastics on horseback – so cool!

7

☐

The judge sits at C in a

__ __ __ __ __ __ __ __

test!

8

☐

The most exciting and challenging phase of eventing is

__ __ __ __ __ -

__ __ __ __ __ __ __ !

9

☐

Rolo's a native pony so his mane is always left unplaited for

__ __ __ __ __ __ __

comps!

10

☐

One, two or four ponies racing with a carriage,

__ __ __ __ __ __ __

is totally epic to watch!

How did you do?
Head to p100 to check your answers!

Popcorn can pull off any
colour, but mint looks the best!

LeMieux
LeMieux

LOOK AFTER YOUR PONY'S...

HOOVES

No foot, no horse! Taking care of your pony's hooves is essential

As pony carers, one of our most important jobs is looking after their hooves! The hoof is a really cool but very complex structure that's responsible for carrying all a pony's weight! Keeping all four hooves in good condition is vital for a pony's wellbeing, as hoof problems can lead to other issues. Plus, healthy hooves mean you'll be able to carry on adventuring!

HEARD IT FROM HARLOW

A farrier is a hoof expert, and your pony should see the farrier every 4–6 weeks, depending on his hoof condition and shoeing cycle.

Perfect Popcorn's feet – so cute!

1. Remember to check your pony's hooves every day. This is way easier if you hang a hoof pick close to his stable or the field gate, because seeing it there will remind you!

2. To pick out your pony's feet, slowly run your hand down his leg and carefully lift up his hoof. Use the pointy side of the pick to remove dirt, taking care around the sensitive frog.

3. Brush the rest of the dirt away – if his hooves are really grubby, grab a bucket of water and stiff brush to give them a good clean so you can easily spot any problems.

THE LOWDOWN

Hooves are made from keratin, which is exactly what makes up your hair and nails, too! It takes a long time for a whole new hoof to grow – between nine and 12 months!

4. Spend time carefully looking at each of your pony's hooves. Check the underside, then gently place the hoof back down on the floor so you can look at the hoof wall.

5. Apply a good quality hoof moisturiser to your pony's feet regularly, ideally every day, and remember to report any issues or worries to your farrier when you see them!

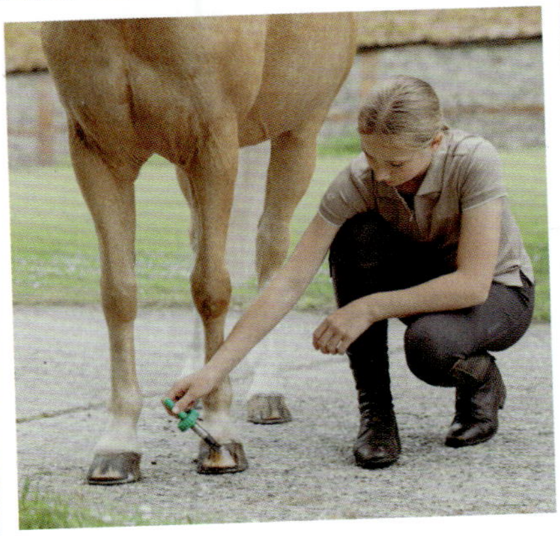

Shiny and strong – winner!

HEARD IT FROM HARLOW

Not all ponies need to wear shoes, and, like Cloudy, some just wear them on their front feet. Shoes help protect the hooves from injury and being worn down really quickly.

Inside out

The best way to support your pony's hoof growth is by making sure he has enough biotin in his diet. Biotin improves the quality of his hooves so they'll be less likely to chip and crack.

You can also apply a moisturising hoof treatment, not one that's just designed to make them shiny.

Healthy from the inside out!

THE LOWDOWN

The triangular-shaped structure on the underside of a pony's hoof is called the frog. It may be small, but it has a mighty role – it helps absorb shock, pumps blood back up the legs to the heart and provides grip.

Ready for inspection

Because hoof problems can take a while to resolve, it's important you spot them quickly! So, keep an eye out for...

- cracks or chips in the hoof wall
- black gunk around the frog
- uneven wear on shoes
- loose nails

No loose shoes here!

> **Remember to report any issues to your farrier**

HEARD IT FROM HARLOW

Some ponies are pros at pulling off shoes in the field when they go zoomies, it's sooo annoying! To help prevent this, you can fit overreach boots – they'll also help reduce the risk of injury.

TOP OF THE CHARTS

These are a few of my favourite things!

MY TOP 5 THINGS TO WATCH...

1. The Kardashians
2. I'm a Celeb!
3. Clarkson's Farm
4. Mean Girls
5. Tangled

MY TOP 5 FOODS...

1. Spag bol
2. Ham and pineapple pizza
3. Green apples
4. Sticky toffee pudding
5. Green grapes

MY TOP 5 SADDLEPAD COLOURS...

1. Walnut
2. Soft mint
3. Azure
4. Chilli
5. Kiwi

MY TOP 5 THINGS TO DO IN MY SPARE TIME...

1. Have a pamper session
2. Read a horsey book
3. Watch the ponies from my bedroom
4. Exercise to help boost my riding!
5. Hang out with my friends, or the ponies!

HEAD OUT ADVENTURING

There's a whole world out there to explore, and what's better than doing it from horseback?

THE LOWDOWN

Wearing high-vis while adventuring is really important for your safety. It means you'll be more visible to others, so be sure to put it on before you head out!

SURF'S UP!

Galloping along the shore with a dreamy sunrise is totally worth the early start. The pics always look incredible and it's literally the best feeling when you can confidently go zoomies across the sand and splash in the sea with your fave pony!

HOME AND AWAY

Spend a rainy day doing some research into the bridlepaths and byways near your yard before heading out – you'll probably find there are way more cool places to explore than you ever realised!

INTO THE WOODS

There's something so peaceful about riding through the woods. Listening to the leaves rustle under your pony's hooves while the leaves dance in the breeze is such a sweet feeling. You can also turn woodland hacks into epic games of I Spy with friends! What can you spot?

HIT THE ROAD

Taking the ponies out in the trailer is not only sooo good for building their confidence in new places, but it also means we can literally go adventuring anywhere we want – as long as it's pony-friendly, of course!

LESSONS LEARNT

Having lessons with an instructor is the best way to supercharge your skills. While it's good to have regular lessons with someone who knows you and your pony well, I've found it sooo useful to have the odd clinic with a pro or new coach – it's done wonders for my riding, plus it means the ponies get to experience somewhere new. Bonus!

Meet COOKIE

FACT FILE

- **SHOW NAME**
  Ystracothi Macsen
- **BREED**
  Welsh Section B
- **COLOUR**
  Liver chestnut
- **BEST FRIEND**
  Popcorn

After months of searching for a Welsh Section B, I found Cookie's advert online when we were driving home from a show one day, and me and my mum instantly fell in love with him! I'd always wanted a liver chestnut pony, too, so it felt like he was going to be the one!

Mum called the breeder straight away and a few days later we went to see him for the first time – before we knew it, he was ours!

He absolutely adores Popcorn and Cloudy, they are all field buddies and it's so cute seeing them together!

Hopes and dreams

Even though he's still young, Cookie has had lots of handling experience with his breeders who have cared for him so well – he's even amazing with the farrier! When he was two years old he won at the Royal Welsh show, so he's been really successful at in-hand showing already!

My goal with Cookie is to do Mountain & Moorland classes, plaited working hunter pony or just flat showing in the native classes, so watch this space! With the amount of talent he's proving to have, along with the loveliest personality, I'm sure we're set for success!

Insider info

Cookie is super greedy! He eats lots of hay and loves all sorts of tasty treats!

> **He absolutely adores Popcorn and Cloudy**

HEARD IT FROM HARLOW

I am obsessed with Cookie's long forelock and the stunning colours in his tail! He loves being fussed over, too, which means he's perfect for me – you know I love a pamper sesh!

I thank my lucky stars every day that Rolo came into my life

4 WAYS PONIES HAVE CHANGED MY LIFE

There are so many more, though!

I've always been pony obsessed, but when Popcorn came into my life it completely changed for the better. I'm so grateful every day for the opportunities the ponies have given me.

Panda loves a crowd!

MEETING MY IDOLS

My YouTube journey has led me to meeting some of the most incredible riders and horses in the world, and I love that I've been able to share it with you all!

SEEING THE WORLD

From local shows to amazing adventures around the globe, I've been lucky enough to travel to loads of top yards and some of the world's most beautiful events!

HEARD IT FROM HARLOW

Just hanging out with ponies can make you feel sooo much better, you don't have to be in the saddle!

SELF BELIEF

You only have to look back at some of my old YouTube videos to see how much my confidence has grown!

TRUE LOVE

Ponies are great listeners and never judge. My boys always put a smile on my face, and they've taught me patience and hard work really does pay off.

"My boys always put a smile on my face"

All about...
CLOUDY

Get to know Cloudy – my speedy little Shetland with a larger than life personality!

PONY PROFILE

- **BREED**
  Shetland
- **HEIGHT**
  10hh
- **COLOUR**
  Cream dun
- **BIRTHDAY**
  15 May 2009

Ideal day...

Cloudy lives his best life whenever he gets to join the big boys for a day out! He loves being the team mascot and whenever he sees the trailer ramp go down, he gets really excited! He's definitely Popcorn, Rolo and Panda's number one supporter!

Dream job...

You guys know from my vlogs that Cloudy has the most mischievous personality, so he'd be a bank robber in another life for sure! His crazy antics certainly keep us on our toes, but we love him for it. It's never a dull day when Cloudy's around!

Favourite memory...

My fave memory with Cloudy has got to be racing together at Badminton Horse Trials in 2023. Riding into the main ring was so nerve-wracking at first, but Cloudy boy loved the atmosphere and we had the best time together – it was epic!

What makes him happy...

Panda – because they are besties! They just love hanging out together, whether that's in the field, on a hack or chilling in the barn. Cloudy always misses Panda when's he out at a competition or off training, but it makes his day when Panda gets home!

JOYFUL JUMPING

You'll be totally in the know with my guide to jumping!

THE LOWDOWN

There are several different equestrian disciplines that involve soaring through the air with your pony! Showjumping, cross-country and working hunter all require your pony to pop over fences but the types of fence, height and difficulty can vary loads, so it's best to start with small, simple jumps to get started.

"The adrenaline when I jump a bigger fence is incredible!"

5 EXERCISES TO TRY...

- [ ] Gridwork – there are tonnes of different layouts to try and you can improve so many skills from a simple grid. From feeling more confident jumping bigger fences to boosting your pony's agility, ask your instructor for some inspo and tips!

- [ ] Riding a course – string a few fences together (or poles on the floor!) and practise riding smooth, accurate lines between them to help your pony jump clear. Ready to make it harder? Add in a double and a few related distances so you can work on your striding!

- [ ] Skinnies are the ultimate test of accuracy and you'll often find them on cross-country and working hunter courses. You'll need to channel your pony straight between your hand and legs to ride them perfectly!

- [ ] Shortening and lengthening strides – being able to seamlessly adjust your pony's canter stride is an essential skill. Set up two poles down the long side around five strides apart, then try opening up and riding four strides by allowing with your hand and squeezing with your legs. Next, ask for six strides by sitting deeper in the saddle to shorten your pony's stride.

- [ ] Jump-off turns – learning to safely cut corners and jump on an angle is key to saving you time on course and helping you work towards that red rosette! Remember to choose your lines carefully – don't turn too tight and guide your pony into the fence with your legs.

4 TIPS FOR THE PERFECT POSITION...

Keep your eyes up and look ahead of you – looking down might cause your pony to drop his shoulder and run out!

Lift yourself out of the saddle slightly and hinge at your hips to fold forward and follow your pony's movement.

Move your hands towards your pony's ears a little to allow him to stretch his head and neck and jump cleanly.

Press your weight down into your heels and keep your lower leg underneath you – if it swings back, you'll become unbalanced!

3 THINGS TO REMEMBER...

The quality of your pony's canter is key – work on a positive, rhythmical canter before you approach a fence!

Don't pick up your jumping position too early! It's best to remain tall until your pony starts to take off.

Introduce your pony to spooky fences gradually to build his confidence. Keep your leg on and a soft rein contact so he can look at the fence, too!

HEARD IT FROM HARLOW

Take your time to warm up ready for your jumping session. Your pony should be tuned into your aids and supple on both reins, so ride lots of transitions, shapes and changes of bend to get him prepped!

2 THINGS TO WEAR...

When going XC, the rules state you must wear a jockey skull and body protector. I like to wear an air jacket, too, for extra protection.

It's a good idea to put boots on your pony when jumping to protect him from knocks!

1 THING I LOVE...

Nailing the perfect stride and achieving that epic feeling as I fly through the air with my pony! I used to get really nervous when jumping, but I've slowly built my confidence and practised loads, which has really improved my skills. The adrenaline when I jump a bigger fence is incredible!

GET READY WITH ME!

Can you crack the code to reveal my pre-ride essentials?

A B C D E F G H I J K L M N O P Q R S T U V W X Y Z

1	2	3	4	5	6	7	8	9	10	11	12	13
	S			T		A	W	C		Y	X	E
14	**15**	**16**	**17**	**18**	**19**	**20**	**21**	**22**	**23**	**24**	**25**	**26**
	B		V				Z		J			Q

		18											
		10											
	9 C	10	6	15 B							15 B		
		25		14							14		
		20		24			2 S		15 B		4		
		4		2 S			7		10		3		
		9 C		18	13 E	7 A	3	9 C	10	1	1	7 A	14
		22					3		5		13 E		
							1		2			2 S	
3	13 E	5 T	7	19	16	1	13 E	14			18	7 A	5
							20					3	
			6	7 A	2	2 S	7	16	13 E	20	7	3	
					20		3					1	
					10			16	1	10	17 V	13 E	2 S
					19								
			14	24	16								
					13 E								

How did you do?
Head to p100 to check your answers!

"Time to head out on another adventure!"

Rocket is just so adorable – he's the perfect addition to our four-legged blond crew!

TIDY UP TIME

Top tidying tips to help keep your kit in order!

Showing products – sorted!

Our yard would be utter mayhem if it wasn't for my amazing cousin Lexi, the Queen of Clean! She absolutely loves a tidying up session and I'm eternally grateful for her obsession with keeping the yard neat and tidy – with five ponies, a busy show schedule and a whole lot of kit, things can get pretty messy!

HEARD IT FROM HARLOW

Sorting my saddlepad collection into colour order is a whole new level of satisfaction. But they have to be arranged by fit and size, too, to make them easier to find!

1. Invest in a good storage unit or trunk, as well as some boxes, to help keep your kit tidy and organised.

2. Sort all your kit into categories. Some rugs, for example, won't be needed in summer so can be packed away. It's handy to keep your daily grooming products by your pony's stable, and have your bathing or show kit elsewhere, ready for when you need it.

3. Give everything a thorough clean up as you organise it all! Wash brushes in warm, soapy water, wipe the outside of bottles and flick off your pony's boots – it's an essential part of the process!

4. Throw away rubbish and other pieces of kit you don't need anymore. Anything that's useful could be donated to a local equine charity or riding school!

5. Don't forget to make a note when things are running out and replace them when supplies are low.

6. Hang up whatever you can! Put rugs on racks, saddlepads on coat hangers and headcollars on hooks!

7. Place small items, such as plaiting bands, in boxes. This keeps them safe and makes them easier to find.

8. Make sure you double check the lids of any lotions and potions are on tight and they're standing upright – you don't want them to leak!

9. Hang up a towel near your stable or in your tack room so you can easily wipe over stirrups, boots and bottles when they get dirty. ☐

10. A label maker is a must! This is the ultimate way to organise your kit as you're sorting through it all. ☐

11. After you've had a good clear out, try to stay on top of your tidying jobs by doing little and often, then it won't be such a chore! ☐

LOOK AFTER YOUR PONY'S...

SKIN AND COAT

Help your pony shine from head to hoof with my tips

Did you know that a smooth, shiny coat is a sign of a healthy pony? Not only do they look stunning when glowing in the sunshine, but it's sooo rewarding to know my hard work looking after them is paying off! Grooming is important, but there's so much more to looking after the ponies' skin and coats than you might think! Find out more right here!

HEARD IT FROM HARLOW

Groom your pony regularly to keep him clean and his coat in top condition. It saves time on show day and means you can spot and deal with any problems quickly!

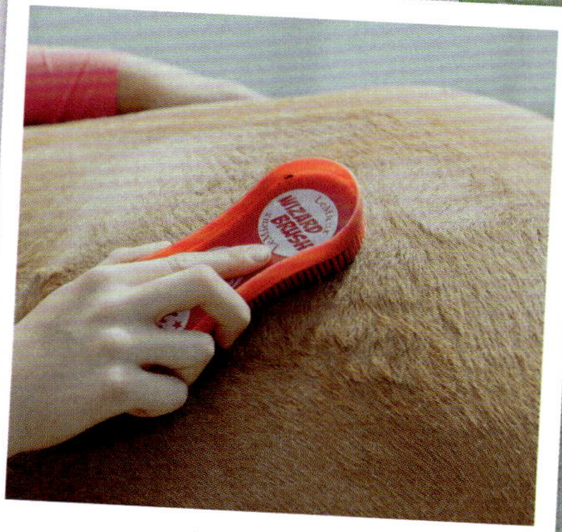

Bye bye, dirt!

1. To lift dirt and dust away from the skin, try using a curry comb in circular motions. It is hands-down the best tool for removing mud and hair when a pony's moulting!

2. To flick away all the remaining dust and loose hairs, I like to use a soft body brush because it really helps to clean up the coat and make the ponies shine!

3. I give my ponies a thorough wash from time to time to cleanse their skin and nourish their coats. This really helps when their coats are changing between seasons, too!

THE LOWDOWN

Did you know it's not the changes in temperature and weather in spring and autumn that affect a pony's coat change? It's actually due to the daylight hours. So clever!

4. Time to get hands on and give your pony a nice massage sesh! He'll love the treatment and it will help stimulate blood flow which will improve the quality of his skin!

5. Regularly feel all over your pony's body and look carefully through his coat for dry skin. Keep an eye out for cuts or grazes, too, as these will need looking after to help them heal!

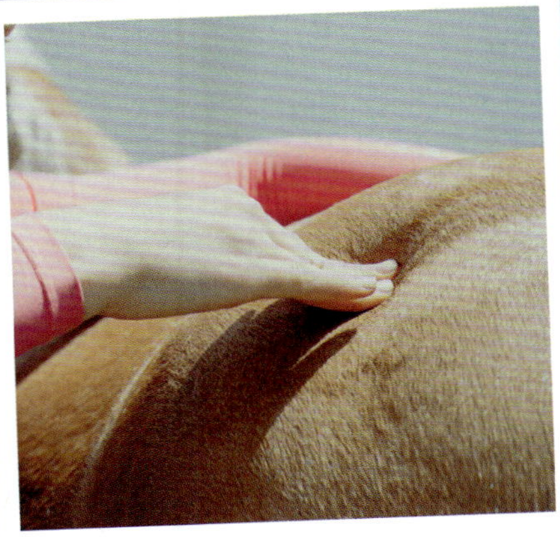

Time for a massage, Popcorn!

THE LOWDOWN

The natural oils produced by the skin make the hair's all over a pony's body water resistant! This means if your pony has a thick coat, it can act like a rug to keep his skin dry. How cool is that?!

HEARD IT FROM HARLOW

Popcorn is our golden boy in summer, but his palomino coat turns milky white in winter – it's crazy how much he changes throughout the year!

Nutrition addition

If your pony has dry or flaky skin, try speaking to your vet and a nutritionist for advice. It could be that he's not getting all the essential vits and mins in his diet, which is affecting his coat condition. Foods that contain oils such as omega 3 are really good for improving skin health, but they can cause weight gain so watch out!

Polishing that golden coat

Take shelter

Rugs are used to help protect your pony's skin from the weather. In summer, fly rugs with UV protection can shield him from the sun's harsh rays, while in very wet weather a waterproof rug can help reduce the risk of bacterial infections like rain scald. Rugs also help keep your pony clean, but don't over-rug him!

Protection on damp days is a must

> **"A curry comb is hands down the best tool for removing mud and hair"**

HEARD IT FROM HARLOW

The ponies' fluffy coats get clipped in winter to help keep them cool during exercise. I like to give them a rub over with a warm, damp cloth and a splash of oil to make them shine.

HORSE PLAY

GO FOR GROUNDWORK

You don't need to ride your pony to keep him strong and supple!

THE LOWDOWN

It's a sensible idea to wear a hat, gloves and sturdy boots when doing groundwork. You should also put your pony's bridle on so you have extra control should he get a bit excited!

POLE PLAYGROUND

Triangles, squares, mazes, fans – there really are loads of different pole layouts to try and I love getting really creative! Working your pony over poles in walk is so good for increasing his awareness of where he's putting each hoof, as well as developing his muscles.

TIME FOR WALKIES

Taking your pony for an in-hand hack is a bit like walking a big dog, but it's the perfect activity for a pony who can't be ridden. Getting out and about will keep both his brain and body busy – plus, it's good exercise for you too!

IN THE LONG RUN

If you've never lunged or long-reined a pony before, it's best to ask an adult to show you how to do it safely and help you get to grips with it! It's a great skill to learn, though, and I've learnt tonnes about how my ponies move from lungeing and long-reining!

AND RELAX...

Stretching is a fab way to prep your pony for his workout and help him relax after a tough session, plus it can help boost your bond! I like to use treats to encourage my ponies to do their yoga poses, and they always feel so supple after it. They also absolutely love the tasty reward!

GHOST BUSTERS

Some ponies are naturally more nervous than others which can make going to new places even more daunting, for both of you! But helping your pony overcome and get past spooky objects from the ground is so good for building his confidence and trust in you.

A TRIP TO THE SPA

Get your pony looking fabulous by treating him to the ultimate Harlow spa session!

Welcome to Harlow's spa, where ponies are given the most luxurious pamper sesh to get them looking and feeling mega! So, if your pony's in need of a spruce-up from head to toe, follow my guide for turning him from muddy monster into a pampered prince!

THE LOWDOWN

Don't fully bath your pony too often because you'll remove all the natural oils that help keep his coat in good condition. It's best to only do it when your pony is really grubby!

1. Grooming

The boys are usually pretty grubby when they come in from the field, especially if they've had a day with no rugs on and a good roll! So, the first part of Harlow's spa day involves a thorough groom to get rid of all the mud and loose hairs – a curry comb is fab for this! At the same time, I pick out their hooves to check for any stones that might've got wedged in.

HEARD IT FROM HARLOW

The boys always get a big spa sesh before a show to make sure they're looking on top form – I can't be having them covered in stains and mud, that certainly won't impress the judges! I also like to use whitening spray to get Panda gleaming!

HEARD IT FROM HARLOW

Solariums are literally one of the best inventions ever! Unless it's a really warm day, I turn on the solarium while I'm bathing and grooming the ponies because it helps keep them warm and their muscles relaxed. Plus, it keeps me warm if it's super chilly!

2. Bathing

Bath time is the best time because it really gets the ponies shining. First, I rinse them all over with the hose to get their coat wet, then apply a good dollop of shampoo to a sponge before working it into the hairs. I like to use a curry comb again here because it gets deeper into the coat to remove dead skin and scurf.

The most important step is the next one – rinsing out all the bubbles! If they aren't washed out, it could make the ponies' skin itchy or sore. Then, when that's all done, I condition the mane and tail to help get rid of the knots and make it silky-smooth.

I like to leave the conditioner in for 10 minutes or so to let it get to work before rinsing out and brushing through! Then, when the boys are all clean, I take them for a hand graze if it's sunny or, if it's cold, I'll pop a cosy rug on that will help dry them off.

3. Trimming

Popcorn's the only one who has a good mane trim from time to time – the others' manes are left more natural because of their breeds. But when Popcorn is due a hairdresser sesh, I often call in my mum for assistance!

We use the handy little trimmers to get rid of any crazy long hairs around his jaw and tidy up his feathers to keep him looking super smart. If your pony is in need of a trim, enlist the help of an adult to make sure you don't give him a dodgy haircut – that would not be a good look!

4. Massaging

The ponies absolutely love a massage, especially Popcorn, and it's so cute when he goes all relaxed and sleepy. This part of Harlow's spa is also a pre-ride essential because it helps get the ponies' blood flowing and muscles prepped for action!

I also like to give the ponies a quick stretch using treats for encouragement. My physio recommends exercises to try, and I've noticed a huge improvement in their flexibility and suppleness!

HEARD IT FROM HARLOW

If I have a show the next day, I always pop a special snuggly hood on the ponies to help prevent them from getting dirty. This is especially important for Panda because he absolutely loves lying in his poo – it's so gross!

> *Bath time is the best time because it really gets the ponies shining*

5. Finishing touches

Harlow's spa day isn't over just yet – the finishing touches are essential! A dollop of hair gloss, a spritz of coat shine and a lick of hoof oil and the ponies are looking their absolute best.

Posing with my best boy!

CAMERA CONFIDENCE

How to feel brave when the lens is focused on you!

Being filmed when riding can be a bit scary at first, especially when you feel like there's pressure to ride your very best all the time, but no one is perfect and it's great fun when you relax into it!

HEARD IT FROM HARLOW

Ask someone who you're used to riding in front of to film you so you can get comfy with the idea of riding when the focus is on you!

COMFORT ZONE

If you're feeling nervous, stick to an activity you're confident with. Don't push yourself out of your comfort zone until you're ready.

DEEP BREATHS

Remember to breathe and smile! Try to keep relaxed by focusing on your breathing pattern – it'll help your pony stay chilled, too!

BENEFIT BOOSTER

Being videoed is really useful for improving your skills, so don't forget that! I always learn loads from watching back videos of me riding!

TIME AGAIN

Practising is the best way to boost your confidence, so ride in front of the camera as much as you can. Why not prop it up on the fence?

All about... PANDA

Get to know Panda – my perfect unicorn who puts his heart and soul into everything!

PONY PROFILE

- **BREED**
  Connemara
- **HEIGHT**
  14.2hh
- **COLOUR**
  Grey
- **BIRTHDAY**
  3 May 2015

Ideal day...

Panda loves spending time in the field, but I reckon his ideal day would be a duvet day, especially if it's raining! Munching on his hay in peace and taking naps in his cosy bed is definitely his dream, even more so if there's a poo pillow to rest on. Gross!

Dream job...

I reckon Panda would be a make-up artist in another life, or maybe a beauty therapist. He's spent a long time perfecting his poo eyeshadow and grass stain blusher – it's a unique vibe, but he rocks it in his own special way – he's so cool!

Favourite memory...

Even though greys are a nightmare to keep clean, I've always dreamt of having one. My best memory so far is the day Panda joined the White family – seeing him walk down the trailer ramp was epic. And I know there are lots more amazing things to come for us!

What makes him happy...

Jumping, for sure! When I first had Panda I hadn't done loads of jumping – it's just not Popcorn's fave thing to do – but now we're sailing over fences and even enjoying Working Hunter together. His big stride and jump make me feel like I'm flying on a real-life unicorn!

WORKING HUNTER WONDERS

Get ready to impress the judges in the show ring!

> *The community spirit in the showing world is amazing!*

THE LOWDOWN

Working hunter is a type of showing class that involves two phases. The first requires you to jump around a course of rustic fences and the second is the individual show.

5 THINGS TO WEAR...

To follow tradition, your riding hat should have a velvet outer, usually black, brown or navy, with a flesh-coloured harness. Fixed peaks are most commonly used, but you can wear a skull cap with a plain velvet or silk hat cover instead.

Most riders wear a classic tweed jacket with canary or beige jodhpurs and a shirt with a stock or tie – it's such a smart, traditional look!

Securing your hair in a hairnet can be a tricky task if it's long, like mine, but it's a must for working hunter classes! Try plaiting it, then tying it in a bun with the hairnet to keep it neat and tidy. You can finish it off with a simple scrunchie for an elegant style.

Depending on your age, the type of horse you're riding and your class rules, you'll either wear jodhpur boots and clips or long, leather boots in black or brown. Don't forget to give them a polish, too, so they're super-clean!

In pony classes you have to wear your body protector for the jumping phase and when warming up over fences so it's a key piece of kit to remember on the day – you don't want to risk not being able to compete!

4 TURNOUT TIPS...

Unless your pony comes under the Mountain and Moorland category, he should be plaited. So, it's time to get practising to enhance his look!

Your pony's tack should be black or brown leather with minimal detailing – avoid blingy browbands and coloured stitching!

Look for a numnah that matches your tack and make sure it fits close to your saddle so it doesn't distract the judge's eye.

Put front boots on your pony for the jumping phase (hind boots aren't allowed) to protect his legs, but remember to remove them for the individual show!

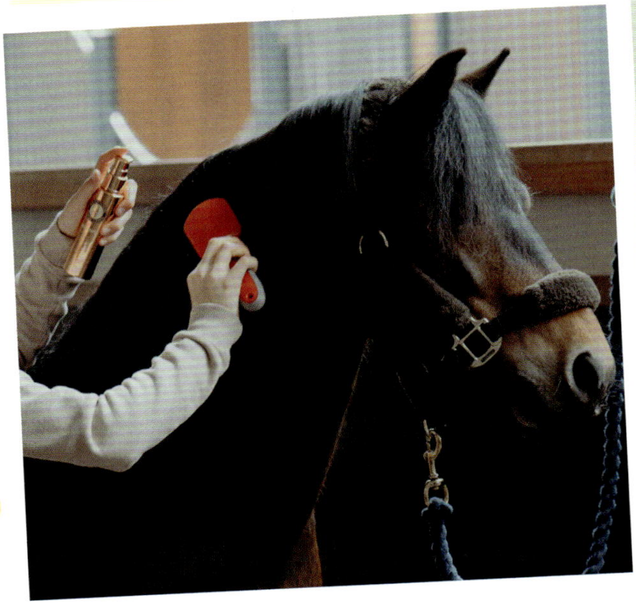

3 THINGS THE JUDGES ARE LOOKING FOR...

Good manners! If your pony rushes into a jump, or refuses to stand patiently in the line-up you'll be marked down, so work on these skills at home. Remember that handling him on the ground is a key part of your training, too!

Bold jumping style – the judges love it when ponies are bold as well as neat and tidy over fences – plus, you'll get faults for knocking or refusing fences – so think about how to fine-tune your pony's jumping technique at home. You could try using bounces or V-poles!

Ground-covering movement – paying attention to your pony's way of going should be a big part of your training. Your pony should be responsive to your aids, supple and working from his hindquarters and over his back into a contact.

HEARD IT FROM HARLOW

The great thing about showing is that anyone can give it a go and there are classes for everyone at all levels! If jumping's not your thing, you could try first ridden or even fun classes at your local venue such as handsomest gelding – Popcorn would definitely win that one!

2 TIPS FOR EACH PHASE...

Jumping – focus on maintaining your canter rhythm to help you hit the perfect stride to each fence – this will help boost your style marks! It's a good idea to practise the types of fence you'll come across to reduce the likelihood of being caught out!

Individual show – during the gallop, lift yourself out of the saddle slightly to allow your pony to open up his stride and show off his moves! Your salute at the end should be a neat movement, too – no need for a dramatic wave!

1 THING I LOVE...

Working hunter is the perfect combo as it's a mix of showing and jumping – my faves! The community spirit in the showing world is amazing, too, and I love seeing all my pals at shows throughout the season!

SPOT THE

Can you find all 10 differences?

A

DIFFERENCE

B

How did you do?
Head to p100 to check your answers!

Early mornings at the beach before anyone else is about are so much fun!

LOOK AFTER YOUR PONY'S...

LEGS

Take good care of your pony's limbs to keep him happy and healthy

Caring for your pony's legs means doing what you can to help prevent injury. As ponies land over a jump, travel across uneven terrain or run around the field with friends, their legs go through a lot of stress. This means we need to look after them to be able to carry on having fun! Check out these awesome facts and tips!

HEARD IT FROM HARLOW

When a horse is born, their legs are 80-90% of the length they'll be when they're fully grown! Isn't that amazing?!

Panda needs extra TLC when he's worked hard

1. Know what's normal for your pony so you can quickly deal with any issues. This is especially important after he's worked hard or has been in the field playing with friends!

2. Starting at the top of your pony's leg, slowly run your hands down both sides all the way to his hoof. If you feel anything different, or spot new cuts or bumps, speak to an adult.

3. You can protect your pony's legs from knocks during exercise and travelling with boots! There are lots of styles, designed for different activities.

THE LOWDOWN

There are no muscles in a pony's lower legs. It's an awesome system of tendons and ligaments that supports his whole bodyweight and help him reach super-fast speeds!

4. Boots that are too tight or too loose can cause damage, so get an adult to check the fit. For most boots, you should be able to fit a finger comfortably down the side.

5. Remember to remove your pony's boots as soon as possible after he's been ridden to stop heat building up, and always thoroughly cool down his legs after exercise, too!

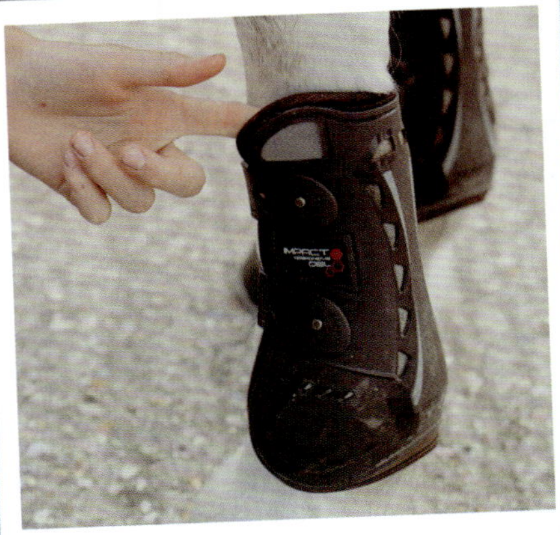

Yep, just right for Panda pops!

THE LOWDOWN

If a pony is resting a front leg, it can be a sign of lameness. However, in the hindlegs it's a little more confusing because the resting can mean relaxing or injury!

HEARD IT FROM HARLOW

Around 60% of a pony's weight is taken on his front legs! This increases to approximately two and a half times his weight when landing from a jump – woah!

Stay cool

Tendons get really warm during intense exercise, so to help keep them healthy and protect your pony from injury, use breathable boots and cool his legs after riding! A good walk off period, followed by hosing until cool to the touch is the best practice. Or you can use special cooling gel or ice boots!

I take off boots as soon as I can

Mud mayhem

Some ponies can suffer from a bacterial infection called mud fever. It's best to avoid washing your pony's legs off if they're muddy. Instead, leave them to dry then brush the mud off! You can also buy boots to protect his legs if the fields are super muddy in winter.

No signs of mud fever – phew!

You can protect your pony's legs from knocks with boots!

HEARD IT FROM HARLOW

Take care of your pony's legs by avoiding riding on deep or rutted ground and trotting on the roads as this can jar his legs and make them sore.

HORSE PLAY

LET YOUR PONY CHOOSE

Like an epic game of this or that, it's time to let your pony control your day!

THE LOWDOWN

Don't let your pony take control if it's not safe. For example, if there's a track he wants to go down but the footing isn't safe, be the boss and redirect him along a pony-friendly path.

DRESSED TO IMPRESS

Pink, blue, green, purple or red – which matchy set will your pony choose for today's outfit? Place two options in front of him and whichever one he sniffs first is the winner! Or, if you fancy a bit of mix 'n' match, you could let him choose the colour of each item to make a crazy, colourful outfit.

EN ROUTE

Going on an adventure with your four-legged friend, but can't decide which route to take? Let your pony choose! It's so funny seeing which way the ponies want to go when they have a longer rein. Towards the gallop field is usually Popcorn's choice!

PADDOCK PLAY

Instead of bringing your pony in from the field at his usual time, why not see if you could let him hang out with his pals and enjoy some grazing time for a little longer? I love doing this, but always stay nearby until they're ready to come in for dinner time!

TASTY TREAT

One thing's for sure – my boys looove their treats and I try to only give them a snack when they've earned it, but sometimes I just can't resist. When we play this or that, I always try to guess which one they will go for before I put two different treats on the floor for them to gobble up!

SCRUB UP

Time for the ponies to have a Harlow spa sesh, and what better way to give them the ultimate treatment by letting them choose which products I use to get them looking amazing? Shampoo, brushes, finishing sprays – whichever item they choose, I'll use!

The yearbook quiz!

How much do you know about me and my ponies?

1 **How tall is Popcorn?**

----

2 **What country did me and my mum visit for a safari?**

----

3 **What time do the ponies have their breakfast?**

----

4 **Who is Rocket's best friend?**

----

5 **Where does Rocket love to be tickled?**

----

6 **What is Harlen's fave riding activity?**

----

7 **What colour is Rolo?**

----

8 **What year was Rolo born?**

How did you do?
Head to p100 to check your answers!

9 **What's my favourite thing to eat?**

---

10 **What breed is Cloudy?**

---

11 **What month was Cloudy born in?**

---

12 **How tall is Panda?**

---

13 **What makes Panda happy?**

---

14 **Which pony have I owned the longest?**

Check out the super-smooth arena!

Cloudy loves a pamper!

BEHIND THE SCENES

My third yearbook and definitely the most fun shoot so far!

HEARD IT FROM HARLOW

Cloudy was a pro all day

HEARD IT FROM HARLOW

So chuffed when the shoot list said 'zoomies'

I think pink's your colour, Cloudy boy!

It takes a village to make a book!

Popcorn loved watching from his stable!

HEARD IT FROM HARLOW

So proud of the boys!

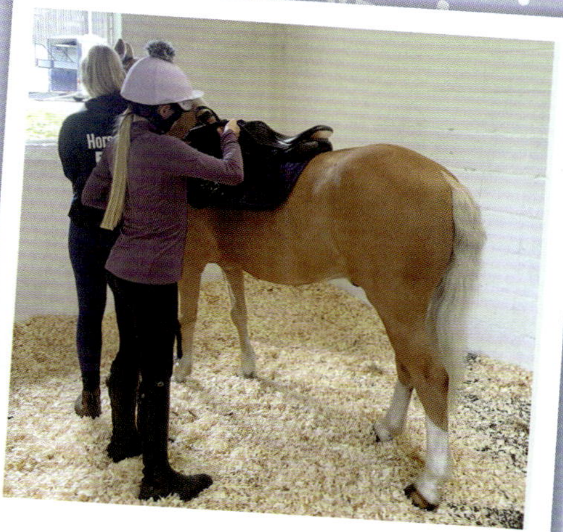

Let's ride!

HEARD IT FROM HARLOW

Sarah sneaking a cuddle with Cloudy

That's a wrap!

Ready to head home!

THE QUIZ

P12 Criss-cross

P38 Discipline decisions

X	E	E	Z	W	Y	K	R	D	V	I	U	W	J	Q
I	L	S	U	K	U	H	X	A	X	G	A	V	R	Y
A	D	R	E	S	S	A	G	E	C	H	H	O	C	F
H	A	F	B	K	T	Z	U	X	Q	I	I	D	R	N
Z	A	K	H	F	Q	C	N	E	C	K	N	K	O	B
D	G	S	H	O	W	J	U	M	P	I	N	G	S	M
N	P	N	E	N	R	D	R	I	V	I	N	G	S	S
Q	P	I	J	D	R	S	N	R	T	A	L	V	C	H
Z	O	O	L	B	O	Z	E	T	G	L	P	A	O	O
C	Z	Z	L	T	B	W	F	B	Q	E	O	U	U	W
K	R	G	U	O	Q	G	B	I	A	Q	B	L	N	I
V	R	M	Z	D	C	N	J	Y	U	L	N	T	T	N
F	R	A	H	O	H	R	G	F	K	B	L	I	R	G
D	R	F	A	J	T	V	U	U	X	U	O	N	Y	R
X	E	N	D	U	R	A	N	C	E	U	X	G	Y	Q

1. Polo
2. Endurance
3. Horseball
4. Racing
5. Showjumping
6. Vaulting
7. Dressage
8. Cross-country
9. Showing
10. Driving

ANSWERS

P62 Get ready with me!

		h[18]											
		o[10]											
	c[9]	o[10]	m[6]	b[15]							b[15]		
		f[25]		r[14]							r[14]		
		p[20]		u[24]			s[2]		b[15]		i[4]		
		i[4]		s[2]			a[7]		o[10]		d[3]		
		c[9]		h[18]	e[13]	a[7]	d[3]	c[9]	o[10]	l[1]	l[1]	a[7]	r[14]
		k[22]					d[3]		t[5]		e[13]		
							l[1]		s[2]			s[2]	
d[3]	e[13]	t[5]	a[7]	n[19]	g[16]	l[1]	e[13]	r[14]			h[18]	a[7]	t[5]
							p[20]					d[3]	
			m[6]	a[7]	s[2]	s[2]	a[7]	g[16]	e[13]	p[20]	a[7]	d[3]	
					p[20]		d[3]					l[1]	
					o[10]			g[16]	l[1]	o[10]	v[17]	e[13]	s[2]
					n[19]								
			r[14]	u[24]	g[16]								
					e[13]								

P86 Spot the difference

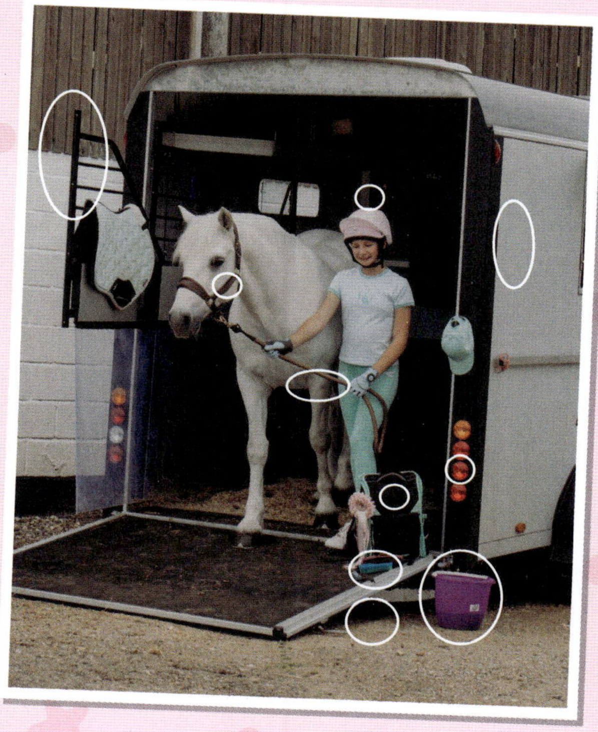

P96 The yearbook quiz!

1. 13.2hh
2. South Africa
3. 7am
4. Harlen
5. Tummy
6. Hacking
7. Brown
8. 2014
9. Spag bol
10. Shetland
11. May
12. 14.2hh
13. Jumping
14. Popcorn